By Derek Walcott

Midsummer

DEREK

WALCOTT

MIDSUMMER

Farrar / Straus / Giroux

NEW YORK

Copyright © 1981, 1982, 1983, 1984 by Derek Walcott
All rights reserved
Published simultaneously in Canada by
Collins Publishers, Toronto
Printed in the United States of America
Designed by Cynthia Krupat
First edition, 1984
Library of Congress Cataloging in Publication Data
Walcott, Derek. | Midsummer.
I. Title
PR9272.9.W3M5 1984   811   83–11563

Acknowledgments are made to The Agni Review,
Bostonia Magazine, Embers, The Harvard Advocate,
The Nation, The New York Review of Books,
The New York Times Magazine, The Pacific
Quarterly Moana, Persea, *and* Trinidad and
Tobago Review, *where some of these poems*
originally appeared. "Tropic Zone" (XLIII),
XXVIII (as "Midsummer"), and
XXXIX (as "The Hare") appeared
originally in The New Yorker

for Elizabeth and Anna

PART ONE

The jet bores like a silverfish through volumes of cloud—
clouds that will keep no record of where we have passed,
nor the sea's mirror, nor the coral busy with its own
culture; they aren't doors of dissolving stone,
but pages in a damp culture that come apart.
So a hole in their parchment opens, and suddenly, in a vast
dereliction of sunlight, there's that island known
to the traveller Trollope, and the fellow traveller Froude,
for making nothing. Not even a people. The jet's shadow
ripples over green jungles as steadily as a minnow
through seaweed. Our sunlight is shared by Rome
and your white paper, Joseph. Here, as everywhere else,
it is the same age. In cities, in settlements of mud,
light has never had epochs. Near the rusty harbor
around Port of Spain bright suburbs fade into words—
Maraval, Diego Martin—the highways long as regrets,
and steeples so tiny you couldn't hear their bells,
nor the sharp exclamations of whitewashed minarets
from green villages. The lowering window resounds
over pages of earth, the canefields set in stanzas.
Skimming over an ocher swamp like a fast cloud of egrets
are nouns that find their branches as simply as birds.
It comes too fast, this shelving sense of home—
canes rushing the wing, a fence; a world that still stands as
the trundling tires keep shaking and shaking the heart.

Companion in Rome, whom Rome makes as old as Rome,
old as that peeling fresco whose flaking paint
is the clouds, you are crouched in some ancient pensione
where the only new thing is paper, like young St. Jerome
with his rock vault. Tonsured, you're muttering a line
that your exiled country will soon learn by heart,
to a flaking, sunlit ledge where a pigeon gurgles.
Midsummer's furnace casts everything in bronze.
Traffic flows in slow coils, like the doors of a baptistry,
and even the kitten's eyes blaze with Byzantine icons.
That old woman in black, unwrinkling your sheet with a palm,
her home is Rome, its history is her house.
Every Caesar's life has shrunk to a candle's column
in her saucer. Salt cleans their bloodstained togas.
She stacks up the popes like towels in cathedral drawers;
now in her stone kitchen, under the domes of onions,
she slices a light, as thick as cheese, into epochs.
Her kitchen wall flakes like an atlas where, once,
Ibi dracones was written, where unchristened cannibals
gnawed on the dry heads of coconuts as Ugolino did.
Hell's hearth is as cold as Pompeii's. We're punished by bells
as gentle as lilies. Luck to your Roman elegies
that the honey of time will riddle like those of Ovid.
Corals up to their windows in sand are my sacred domes,
gulls circling a seine are the pigeons of my St. Mark's,
silver legions of mackerel race through our catacombs.

At the Queen's Park Hotel, with its white, high-ceilinged rooms,
I reenter my first local mirror. A skidding roach
in the porcelain basin slides from its path to Parnassus.
Every word I have written took the wrong approach.
I cannot connect these lines with the lines in my face.
The child who died in me has left his print on
the tangled bed linen, and it was his small voice
that whispered from the gargling throat of the basin.
Out on the balcony I remember how morning was:
It was like a granite corner in Piero della Francesca's
"Resurrection," the cold, sleeping foot
prickling like the small palms up by the Hilton.
On the dewy Savannah, gently revolved by their grooms,
snorting, delicate-ankled racehorses exercise,
as delicate-ankled as brown smoke from the bakeries.
Sweat darkens their sides, and dew has frosted the skins
of the big American taxis parked all night on the street.
In black asphalt alleys marked by a ribbon of sunlight,
the closed faces of shacks are touched by that phrase in
    Traherne:
"The corn was orient and immortal wheat,"
and the canefields of Caroni. With all summer to burn,
a breeze strolls down to the docks, and the sea begins.

This Spanish port, piratical in diverseness,
with its one-eyed lighthouse, this damned sea of noise,
this ocher harbor, mantled by its own scum,
offers, from white wrought-iron balconies,
the nineteenth-century view. You can watch it become
more African hourly—crusted roofs, hot as skillets
peppered with cries; between fast-fry wagons,
floating seraphic Muslims cannot make it hush.
By the pitch of noon, the one thing wanting
is a paddle-wheeler with its rusty parrot's scream,
whistling in to be warped, and Mr. Kurtz on the landing.
Stay on the right bank in the imperial dream—
the Thames, not the Congo. From the small-island masts
of the schooner basin to the plate-glass fronts
of the Holiday Inn is one step, and from need to greed
through the river of clogged, circling traffic is
a few steps more. The world had no time to change
to a doorman's braid from the loincloths of Africa.
So, when the stores draw their blinds, like an empire's ending,
and the banks fade like the peaks of the Hindu Kush,
a cloaked wind, bent like a scavenger, rakes the trash
in the gutters. It is hard not to see the past's
vision of lampposts branching over streets of bush,
the plazas cracked by the jungle's furious seed.

V

The hemispheres lie sweating, flesh to flesh,
on a damp bed. The far ocean grinds in waves
of air-conditioning. The air is scaled like a fish
that leaves dry salt on the hands, and one believes
only in ice, the white zones of refrigerators.
In muslin midsummer along Fourteenth Street, hucksters
with cardboard luggage stacked near the peeling rind
of advertisements have made the Big Apple a mango;
shy as wallflowers at first, the dazed high-rises
rock to reggae and salsa; democracy's price is
two steps forward and three steps back in the Aztec tango
of assimilation, with no bar to the barrio.
On Fridays, an exodus crawls to the Hamptons.
Spit dries on the lips of the curb, and sweat
makes the furniture float away in islands.
Walk the breezy scrub dunes from Montauk to Amagansett,
while the salt of the earth turns into dirt in the cities. The vista
in dusty travel windows blooms with umbrellas
that they cannot go back to. Rats, biting the hands
that fed them. In that drugged dance of dealers,
remote-controlled by a Walkman like he can't stop,
Jesus propositions a seersucker suit, "Hey, mister,
just a sec . . ." The thumb of an Irish cop
rolls his bullets like beads. Glued to his own transistor.

Midsummer stretches beside me with its cat's yawn.
Trees with dust on their lips, cars melting down
in its furnace. Heat staggers the drifting mongrels.
The capitol has been repainted rose, the rails
round Woodford Square the color of rusting blood.
Casa Rosada, the Argentinian mood,
croons from the balcony. Monotonous lurid bushes
brush the damp clouds with the ideograms of buzzards
over the Chinese groceries. The oven alleys stifle.
In Belmont, mournful tailors peer over old machines,
stitching June and July together seamlessly.
And one waits for midsummer lightning as the armed sentry
in boredom waits for the crack of a rifle.
But I feed on its dust, its ordinariness,
on the faith that fills its exiles with horror,
on the hills at dusk with their dusty orange lights,
even on the pilot light in the reeking harbor
that turns like a police car's. The terror
is local, at least. Like the magnolia's whorish whiff.
All night, the barks of a revolution crying wolf.
The moon shines like a lost button.
The yellow sodium lights on the wharf come on.
In streets, dishes clatter behind dim windows.
The night is companionable, the future as fierce as
tomorrow's sun everywhere. I can understand
Borges's blind love for Buenos Aires,
how a man feels the streets of a city swell in his hand.

Our houses are one step from the gutter. Plastic curtains
or cheap prints hide what is dark behind windows—
the pedalled sewing machine, the photos, the paper rose
on its doily. The porch rail is lined with red tins.
A man's passing height is the same size as their doors,
and the doors themselves, usually no wider than coffins,
sometimes have carved in their fretwork little half-moons.
The hills have no echoes. Not the echo of ruins.
Empty lots nod with their palanquins of green.
Any crack in the sidewalk was made by the primal fault
of the first map of the world, its boundaries and powers.
By a pile of red sand, of seeding, abandoned gravel
near a burnt-out lot, a fresh jungle unfurls its green
elephants' ears of wild yams and dasheen.
One step over the low wall, if you should care to,
recaptures a childhood whose vines fasten your foot.
And this is the lot of all wanderers, this is their fate,
that the more they wander, the more the world grows wide.
So, however far you have travelled, your
steps make more holes and the mesh is multiplied—
or why should you suddenly think of Tomas Venclova,
and why should I care about whatever they did to Heberto
when exiles must make their own maps, when this asphalt
takes you far from the action, past hedges of unaligned flowers?

VIII

A radiant summer, so fierce it turns yellow
like the haze before a holocaust. Like a general,
I arrange lines that must increase its radiance, work
that will ripen with peace, like a gold-framed meadow
in Brueghel or Pissarro. No, let the imagination range wherever
its correspondences take it, let it take its luck
on the roads, a Flemish road fenced with poplars,
or grind with Rimbaud the white shale of Charleroi;
let it come back tired to say that summer is the same
everywhere. Black leaves churn in its bonfires, rooks
clatter from my hair, and where is the difference?
The heart is housebound in books—open your leaves,
let light freckle the earth-colored earth, since
light is plenty to make do with. Midsummer bursts
out of its body, and its poems come unwarranted,
as when, hearing what sounds like rain, we startle a place
where a waterfall crashes down rocks. Abounding grace!

It touches earth, that branched diviner's rod
the lightning, like the swift note of a swallow on the staff
of four electric wires, while everything I read
or write goes on too long. Ah, to have
a tone colloquial and stiff,
the brevity of that short syllable, God,
all synthesis in one heraldic stroke,
like Li Po or a Chinese laundry mark! Walk
these hot streets, their signs a dusty backdrop stuck
to the maundering ego. The lines that jerk
into step do not fit any mold. More than time
keeps shifting. Language never fits geography
except when the earth and summer lightning rhyme.
When I was greener, I strained with a branch
to utter every tongue, language, and life at once.
More skillful now, I'm more dissatisfied.
They never align, nature and your
own nature. Too rapid the lightning's shorthand,
too patient the sea repeatedly tearing up paper,
too frantic the wind unravelling the same knot,
too slow the stones crawling toward language every night.

X

No subtle fugues between black day, black night,
no grays, no subterfuge in this straight light.
A smoky, churning dark, shot with the white-hot pokers
of street lamps. The beast with two backs growls from the bushes,
and the harbor hisses like a whore over its fence.
When sonnets come, they come not single spies but in
battalions. They breed like larvae from your boredom. Sin
finds its own level, so, like a rising fish, you are drawn
to surfaces, passing again the simplified silhouettes
outside hot cinemas. Summer is one-dimensional
as lust, and boredom like a whetstone grinds a knife
or a pen. Above the flat, starlit roofs, ambition
is vertical. You miss the other city's blazing towers,
passing repeated hedges of hibiscus, allamanda, croton.
Walk around the black summer streets like an automaton—
midsummer sticks to your thoughts like a damp shirt.
Your life and your work are here, both transient powers.
In phosphorescent sludge, black schooners
break into silver one last time, as the moon sets.

My double, tired of morning, closes the door
of the motel bathroom; then, wiping the steamed mirror,
refuses to acknowledge me staring back at him.
With the softest grunt, he stretches my throat for the function
of scraping it clean, his dispassionate care
like a barber's lathering a corpse—extreme unction.
The old ritual would have been as grim
if the small wisps that curled there in the basin
were not hairs but minuscular seraphim.
He clips our mustache with a snickering scissors,
then stops, reflecting, in midair. Certain sadnesses
are not immense, but fatal, like the sense of sin
while shaving. And empty cupboards where her dresses
shone. But why flushing a faucet, its vortex
swivelling with bits of hair, could make some men's
hands quietly put aside their razors,
and sense their veins as filth floating downriver
after the dolorous industries of sex,
is a question swans may raise with their white necks,
that the cockerel answers quickly, treading his hens.

XII

To betray philosophy is the gentle treason
of poets, to smile at all science, scorning its instruments;
these lines will wilt like mayflies, or termites butting
a hotel lamp to pile in a dust heap at its pediments,
kamikazes or Icari singed in empirical radiance,
thoughts off-the-cuff scorched in the sight of reason.
How profound were they, anyway, those sheeted blighters,
the Stoics, muttering in their beards what every kid knows,
that to everything there is a time and a season,
that we never enter a river or the same bed twice?
The smokeless fire of time scared Heraclitus—
he saw this hotel lamp, midsummer, and the inner light as
one flame, and staring made his eyes run.
The bathtub of a grave displaces the exact weight in dirt as
Archimedes' arse. Lift up that old Greek skirt,
and every girl sees what philosophy is about.
Genius was not arrested for its epoch-shattering shout
but for running in the streets naked, bearded, full-grown
in its dangling appropriate spheres, spluttering out
that what it discovers was always there to be known.

Today I respect structure, the antithesis of conceit.
The overworked muck of my paintings, my bad plots! But
   always,
when the air is empty, I hear actors talking,
the resonance of what is both ordinary and wise.
Specters multiply with age, the peopled head
is crossed by impatient characters, the ears clamped shut;
behind them I hear the actors mutter and shout—
the lit stage is empty, the set prepared,
and I cannot find the key to let them out.
O Christ, my craft, and the long time it is taking!
Sometimes the flash is seen, a sudden exultation
of lightning fixing earth in its place; the asphalt's skin
smells freshly of childhood in the drying rain.
Then I believe that it is still possible, the happiness
of truth, and the young poet who stands in the mirror
smiles with a nod. He looks beautiful from this distance.
And I hope I am what he saw, an enduring ruin.

With the frenzy of an old snake shedding its skin,
the speckled road, scored with ruts, smelling of mold,
twisted on itself and reentered the forest
where the dasheen leaves thicken and folk stories begin.
Sunset would threaten us as we climbed closer
to her house up the asphalt hill road, whose yam vines
wrangled over gutters with the dark reek of moss,
the shutters closing like the eyelids of that mimosa
called Ti-Marie; then—lucent as paper lanterns,
lamplight glowed through the ribs, house after house—
there was her own lamp at the black twist of the path.
There's childhood, and there's childhood's aftermath.
She began to remember at the minute of the fireflies,
to the sound of pipe water banging in kerosene tins,
stories she told to my brother and myself.
Her leaves were the libraries of the Caribbean.
The luck that was ours, those fragrant origins!
Her head was magnificent, Sidone. In the gully of her voice
shadows stood up and walked, her voice travels my shelves.
She was the lamplight in the stare of two mesmerized boys
still joined in one shadow, indivisible twins.

I can sense it coming from far, too, Maman, the tide
since day has passed its turn, but I still note
that as a white gull flashes over the sea, its underside
catches the green, and I promise to use it later.
The imagination no longer goes as far as the horizon,
but it keeps coming back. At the edge of the water
it returns clean, scoured things that, like rubbish,
the sea has whitened, chaste. Disparate scenes.
The pink and blue chattel houses in the Virgins
in the trade winds. My name caught in
the kernel of my great-aunt's throat.
A yard, an old brown man with a mustache
like a general's, a boy drawing castor-oil leaves in
great detail, hoping to be another Albrecht Dürer.
I have cherished these better than coherence
as the same tide for us both, Maman, comes nearer—
the vine leaves medalling an old wire fence
and, in the shade-freckled yard, an old man like a colonel
under the green cannonballs of a calabash.

So what shall we do for the dead, to whose conch-bordered
tumuli our lifelong attraction is drawn
as to a magnetic empire, whose cities lie ordered
with streets and rational avenues, exact as the grid
of our vibrating metropolis? In our arrogance, we imagine
that they, too, share the immense, inaudible pulse
of the clock-shaped earth, slower than ours, maybe, but within
our dimension, our simple mathematical formulae.
Any peace so indifferent, where all our differences fuse,
is an insult to imagine; what use is any labor we
accept? They must find our prayers boring, for one prays
that they will keep missing us when they have no urge
to be ever-remembered, they cannot see what we hoard—
photograph, letter, keepsake, muttered or knitted homily—
as we change flags and houses. We still wish them to serve
us, expecting from death what we expect of our prayers—
that their hearts lift like ours with the surge
of the surf and the cupolas of the sunset, that the kingfisher
startles their darkness sometimes. But each one prefers
the silence that was his birthright, and the shore
where the others wait neither to end nor begin.

XVII

I pause to hear a racketing triumph of cicadas
setting life's pitch, but to live at their pitch
of joy is unendurable. Turn off
that sound. After the plunge of silence,
the eye gets used to the shapes of furniture, and the mind
to darkness. The cicadas are frantic as my mother's
feet, treading the needles of approaching rain.
Days thick as leaves then, close to each other as hours,
and a sunburnt smell rose up from the drizzled road.
I stitch her lines to mine now with the same machine.
What work lies ahead of us, what sunlight for generations!—
The lemon-rind light in Vermeer, to know it will wait
there for others, the broken eucalyptus
leaf, still sharply smelling of turpentine,
the breadfruit's foliage, rust-edged like van Ruysdael.
The Dutch blood in me is drawn to detail.
I once brushed a drop of water from a Flemish still life
in a book of prints, believing it was real.
It reflected the world in its crystal, quivering with weight.
What joy in that sweat drop, knowing others will persevere!
Let them write, "At fifty he reversed the seasons,
the road of his blood sang with the chattering cicadas,"
as when I took to the road to paint in my eighteenth year.

XVIII

In the other 'eighties, a hundred midsummers gone
like the light of domestic paradise, the hedonist's
idea of heaven was a French kitchen's sideboard,
apples and clay carafes from Chardin to the Impressionists;
art was *une tranche de vie*, cheese or home-baked bread—
light, in their view, was the best that time offered.
The eye was the only truth, and whatever traverses
the retina fades when it darkens; the depth of *nature morte*
was that death itself is only another surface
like the canvas, since painting cannot capture thought.
A hundred midsummers gone, with the rippling accordion,
bustled skirts, boating parties, zinc-white strokes on water,
girls whose flushed cheeks wouldn't outlast their roses.
Then, like dried-up tubes, the coiled soldiers
piled up on the Somme, and Verdun. And the dead
less real than a spray burst of chrysanthemums,
the identical carmine for still life and for the slaughter
of youth. They were right—everything becomes
its idea to the painter with easel rifled on his shoulders.

Gauguin / i

On the quays of Papeete, the dawdling white-ducked colonists
drinking with whores whose skin is the copper of pennies
pretend, watching the wild skins of the light and shade,
that a straight vermouth re-creates the metropolis,
but the sun has scorched those memories from my head—
Cézanne bricking in color, each brick no bigger than a square
    inch,
the pointillists' dots like a million irises.
I saw in my own cheekbones the mule's head of a Breton,
the placid, implacable strategy of the Mongol,
the mustache like the downturned horns of a helmet;
the chain of my blood pulled me to darker nations,
though I looked like any other sallow, crumpled colon
stepping up to the pier that day from the customs launch.
I am Watteau's wild oats, his illegitimate heir.
Get off your arses, you clerks, and find your fate,
the devil's prayer book is the hymn of patience,
grumbling in the fog. Pack, leave! I left too late.

ii

I have never pretended that summer was paradise,
or that these virgins were virginal; on their wooden trays
are the fruits of my knowledge, radiant with disease,
and they offer you this, in their ripe sea-almond eyes,
their clay breasts glowing like ingots in a furnace.
No, what I have plated in amber is not an ideal, as
Puvis de Chavannes desired it, but corrupt—
the spot on the ginger lily's vulva, the plantain's phalloi,
the volcano that chafes like a chancre, the lava's smoke
that climbs to the sibilant goddess with its hiss.
I have baked the gold of their bodies in that alloy;
tell the Evangelists paradise smells of sulphur,
that I have felt the beads in my blood erupt
as my brush stroked their backs, the cervix
of a defrocked Jesuit numbering his chaplet.
I placed a blue death mask there in my Book of Hours
that those who dream of an earthly paradise may read it
as men. My frescoes in sackcloth to the goddess Maya.
The mangoes redden like coals in a barbecue pit,
patient as the palms of Atlas, the papaya.

Watteau

The amber spray of trees feather-brushed with the dusk,
the ruined cavity of some spectral château, the groin
of a leering satyr eaten with ivy. In the distance, the grain
of some unreapable, alchemical harvest, the hollow at
the heart of all embarkations. Nothing stays green
in that prodigious urging toward twilight;
in all of his journeys the pilgrims are in fever
from the tremulous strokes of malaria's laureate.
So where is Cythera? It, too, is far and feverish,
it dilates on the horizon of his near-delirium, near
and then further, it can break like the spidery rigging
of his ribboned barquentines, it is as much nowhere
as these broad-leafed islands, it is the disease
of elephantine vegetation in Baudelaire,
the tropic bug in the Paris fog. For him, it is the mirror
of what is. Paradise is life repeated spectrally,
an empty chair echoing the emptiness.

A long, white, summer cloud, like a cleared linen table,
makes heaven emptier, like after-dinner Sundays
when the Bible begs to be lifted, and the old terrifying verses
raise a sandstorm and bone-white Palestinian rocks
where a ram totters for purchase, bleating like Isaiah.
Dry rage of the desert fathers that scared a child,
the Baptist crying by the cracked river basin, curses
that made the rose an intellectual fire.
Through the skull's stone eyes, the radiant logwood
consumes this August, and a white sun sucks
sweat from the desert. A shadow marks the Word.
I have forgotten a child's hope of the resurrection,
bodies locked up in musting cupboard drawers
among the fish knives and the napery (all the dead earth holds),
to be pulled open at the hour of our birth—
the cloud waits in emptiness for the apostles,
for the fruit, wine amphoras, mutton on groaning trestles,
but only the servant knows heaven is still possible,
some freckled Martha, radiant, dependable,
singing a hymn from your childhood while she folds
her Saviour like a white napkin in the earth.

Rest, Christ! from tireless war. See, it's midsummer,
but what roars in the throat of the oaks is martial man,
the marching hosannas darken the wheat of Russia,
the coiled ram hides in the rocks of Afghanistan.
Crowned hydrants gush, baptizing the street urchins,
the water cannons blot their screams in mist,
but snow does not melt from the furnace brow of Mahomet,
or napkins hemorrhage from the brow of Christ.
Along the island the almonds seethe with anger,
the wind that churns these orchards of white surf
and whistles dervishes up from the hot sand
revolves this globe, this painted O that spins,
reciting as it moves, tribes, frontiers,
dots that are sounds, cities that love their names,
while weather vanes still scrape the sky for omens.
Though they have different sounds for "God" or "hunger,"
the opposing alphabets in city squares
shout with one voice, nation takes on nation,
and, from their fury of pronunciation,
children lie torn on rubble for a noun.

XXIII

With the stampeding hiss and scurry of green lemmings,
midsummer's leaves race to extinction like the roar
of a Brixton riot tunnelled by water hoses;
they seethe toward autumn's fire—it is in their nature,
being men as well as leaves, to die for the sun.
The leaf stems tug at their chains, the branches bending
like Boer cattle under Tory whips that drag every wagon
nearer to apartheid. And, for me, that closes
the child's fairy tale of an antic England—fairy rings,
thatched cottages fenced with dog roses,
a green gale lifting the hair of Warwickshire.
I was there to add some color to the British theater.
"But the blacks can't do Shakespeare, they have no experience."
This was true. Their thick skulls bled with rancor
when the riot police and the skinheads exchanged quips
you could trace to the Sonnets, or the Moor's eclipse.
Praise had bled my lines white of any more anger,
and snow had inducted me into white fellowships,
while Calibans howled down the barred streets of an empire
that began with Caedmon's raceless dew, and is ending
in the alleys of Brixton, burning like Turner's ships.

XXIV

What broke the green lianas' ropes? Scaled armor.
What folded the bittern in midflight? One arrow.
What flapped the mackerel agape into quiet? A lancer.
Who flew level as morning? The sea sparrow.
Yes, the sea swift flew nameless that wordless summer
in the leafy silence before their christening language.
The berry leaf died of its own accord, as always, and
the parakeet screeched its own question and answer,
the right verb leapt like a fish from its element,
the tadpole wriggled like an eager comma,
and the snake coiled round its trunk in an ampersand.
It was the snake that linked two hemispheres,
since in the world's bitter half of churches and domes
another new epoch groaned, opening on its hinge;
from his balcony another monarch pronounced a new age
as gargoyles shifted their haunches with a fixed grimace;
in an alley another throat was opened by a cutpurse
like the valve of an oyster. Was evil brought to this place
with language? Did the sea worm bury that secret in clear sand,
in the coral cathedrals, the submarine catacombs
where the jellyfish trails its purple, imperial fringe?

The sun has fired my face to terra-cotta.
It carries the heat from his kiln all through the house.
But I cherish its wrinkles as much as those on blue water.
Gnats drill little holes around a saw-toothed cactus,
a furnace has curled the knives of the oleander,
and a branch of the logwood blurs with wild characters.
A stone house waits on the steps. Its white porch blazes.
I tell you a promise brought to me by the surf:
You shall see transparent Helen pass like a candle
flame in sunlight, weightless as woodsmoke that hazes
the sand with no shadow. My palms have been sliced by the
    twine
of the craft I have pulled at for more than forty years.
My Ionia is the smell of burnt grass, the scorched handle
of a cistern in August squeaking to rusty islands;
the lines I love have all their knots left in.
Through the stunned afternoon, when it's too hot to think
and the muse of this inland ocean still waits for a name,
and from the salt, dark room, the tight horizon line
catches nothing, I wait. Chairs sweat. Paper crumples the floor.
A lizard gasps on the wall. The sea glares like zinc.
Then, in the door light: not Nike loosening her sandal,
but a girl slapping sand from her foot, one hand on the frame.

Before that thundercloud breaks from its hawsers,
those ropes of rain, a wind makes the sea grapes wince,
and the reef signals its last flash of lime.
Feeling her skin cool, the housemaid August
runs into the yard to pull down clouds, like a laundress,
from the year's meridian, her mouth stuffed with wooden pins.
She's seen these flashes of quartz, she knows it's time
for the guests on the beach to come up to the house,
and, hosing sand from scorched feet, let the hinges rust
in holes for another year. But an iron band
still binds their foreheads: the bathers stand
begging the dark clouds, whose spinnakers race over the dunes,
for one more day. Here, the salt vine dries
as fast as it grows, and before you look, a year's gone
with your shadow. The temperate homilies can't
take root in sand; the cicada can fiddle his tunes
all year, if he likes, to the twig-brown ant.
The cloud passes high like a god staying his powers—
the pocked sand dries, umbrellas reopen like flowers—
but those who measure midsummer by a year's trials
have felt a chill grip an ankle. They put down their books
) count the children crouched over pools, and the idolaters
angling themselves to the god's face, like sundials.

Certain things here are quietly American—
that chain-link fence dividing the absent roars
of the beach from the empty ball park, its holes
muttering the word umpire instead of empire;
the gray, metal light where an early pelican
coasts, with its engine off, over the pink fire
of a sea whose surface is as cold as Maine's.
The light warms up the sides of white, eager Cessnas
parked at the airstrip under the freckling hills
of St. Thomas. The sheds, the brown, functional hangar,
are like those of the Occupation in the last war.
The night left a rank smell under the casuarinas,
the villas have fenced-off beaches where the natives walk,
illegal immigrants from unlucky islands
who envy the smallest polyp its right to work.
Here the wetback crab and the mollusc are citizens,
and the leaves have green cards. Bulldozers jerk
and gouge out a hill, but we all know that the dust
is industrial and must be suffered. Soon—
the sea's corrugations are sheets of zinc
soldered by the sun's steady acetylene. This
drizzle that falls now is American rain,
stitching stars in the sand. My own corpuscles
are changing as fast. I fear what the migrant envies:
the starry pattern they make—the flag on the post office—
the quality of the dirt, the fealty changing under my foot.

Something primal in our spine makes the child swing
from the gnarled trapeze of a sea-almond branch.
I have been comparing the sea almond's shapes to the suffering
in van Gogh's orchards. And that, too, is primal. A bunch
of sea grapes hangs over the calm sea. The shadows
I shovel with a dry leaf are as warm as ash, as
noon jerks toward its rigid, inert center.
Sunbathers broil on their grid, the shallows they enter
are so warm that out in the reef the blear grouper lunges
at nothing, teased by self-scaring minnows.
Abruptly remembering its job, a breaker glazes
the sand that dries fast. For hours, without a heave,
the sea suspires through the deep lungs of sponges.
In the thatched beach bar, a clock tests its stiff elbow
every minute and, outside, an even older iguana
climbs hand over claw, as unloved as Quasimodo,
into his belfry of shade, swaying there. When a
cloud darkens, my terror caused it. Lizzie and Anna
lie idling on different rafts, their shadows under them.
The curled swell has the clarity of lime.
In two more days my daughters will go home.
The frame of human happiness is time,
the child's swing slackens to a metronome.
Happiness sparkles on the sea like soda.

Perhaps if I'd nurtured some divine disease,
like Keats in eternal Rome, or Chekhov at Yalta,
something that sharpened the salt fragrance of sweat
with the lancing nib of my pen, my gift would increase,
as the hand of a cloud turning over the sea will alter
the sunlight—clouds smudged like silver plate,
leaves that keep trying to summarize my life.
Under the brain's white coral is a seething anthill.
You had such a deep faith in that green water, once.
The skittering fish were harried by your will—
the stingray halved itself in clear bottom sand,
its tail a whip, its back as broad as a shovel;
the sea horse was fragile as glass, like grass, every tendril
of the wandering medusa: friends and poisons.
But to curse your birthplace is the final evil.
You could map my limitations four yards up from a beach—
a boat with broken ribs, the logwood that grows only thorns,
a fisherman throwing away fish guts outside his hovel.
What if the lines I cast bulge into a book
that has caught nothing? Wasn't it privilege
to have judged one's work by the glare of greater minds,
though the spool of days that midsummer's reel rewinds
comes bobbling back with its question, its empty hook?

PART TWO

XXX

Gold dung and urinous straw from the horse garages,
click-clop of hooves sparking cold cobblestone.
From bricked-in carriage yards, exhaling arches
send the stale air of transcendental Boston—
tasselled black hansoms trotting under elms,
tilting their crops to the shade of Henry James.
I return to the city of my exile down Storrow Drive,
the tunnel with its split seraphs flying *en face,*
with finite sorrow; blocks long as paragraphs
pass in a style to which I'm not accustomed,
since, if I were, I would have been costumed
to drape the cloaks of couples who arrive
for dinner, drawing their chairs from tables where each glass,
catching the transcendental clustered lights,
twirled with perceptions. Style is character—
so my forehead crusts like brick, my sockets char
like a burnt brownstone in the Negro Quarter;
but when a fog obscures the Boston Common
and, up Beacon Hill, the old gas standards stutter
to save their period, I see a black coachman,
with gloves as white as his white-ankled horse,
who counts their laughter, their lamplit good nights,
then jerks the reins of his brass-handled hearse.

Along Cape Cod, salt crannies of white harbors,
white spires, white filling stations, the orthodox
New England offering of clam-and-oyster bars,
like drying barnacles leech harder to their docks
as their day ebbs. Colonies of dark seamen,
whose ears were tuned to their earringed ancestors'
hymn of the Mediterranean's ground bass,
thin out like flocks of some endangered species,
their gutturals, like a parched seal's, on the rocks.
High on the hillsides, the crosstrees of pines
endure the Sabbath with the nerves of aspens.
They hear the Pilgrim's howl changed from the sibyl's,
that there are many nations but one God,
black hat, black-suited with his silver buckle,
damning the rock pool for its naiad's chuckle,
striking this coast with his priapic rod.
A chilling wind blows from my Methodist childhood.
The Fall is all around us—it is New England's
hellfire sermon, and my own voice grows hoarse in
the fog whose bellowing horn is the sea siren's:
a trawler groping from the Port of Boston,
snow, mixed with steam, blurring the thought of islands.

XXXII

The sirens will keep on singing, they will never break
the flow of their one-voiced river to proselytize:
"Come back, come back!"; your head will roll like the others,
the rusted, open-mouthed tins with their Orphic cries.
The city of Boston will not change for your sake.
Cal's bulk haunts my classes. The shaggy, square head tilted,
the mist of heated affection blurring his glasses,
slumped, but the hands repeatedly bracketing vases
of air, the petal-soft voice that has never wilted—
its flowers of illness carpet the lanes of Cambridge,
and the germ of madness is here. Tonight, on the news,
some black kids, one bandaged, were escorted with drawn baton
to police cars. The slicing light on their hoods
divides the spitters from those who should be spat on,
keeping a red eye on colored neighborhoods.
The sirens go on singing, while Lowell's head
rolls past the Harvard boathouse, and his Muse
roars for the Celtics in the Irish bars.
They move in schools, erect, pale fishes in streets;
transparent, fish-eyed, they skitter when I divide,
like a black porpoise heading for the straits,
and the sirens keep singing in their echoing void.

XXXIII

[for Robert Fitzgerald]

Those grooves in that forehead of sand-colored flesh
were cut by declining keels, and the crow's foot
that prints an asterisk by unburied men
reminds him how many more by the Scamander's
gravel fell and lie waiting for their second fate.
Who next should pull his sword free of its mesh
of weeds and hammer at the shield
of language till the wound and the word fit?
A whole war is fought backward to its cause.
Last night, the Trojan and the Greek commanders
stood up like dogs when his strange-smelling shadow
hung loitering round their tents. Now, at sunrise,
the dead begin to cough, each crabwise hand
feels for its lance, and grips it like his pen.
A helmsman drowns in an inkblot, an old man wanders
a pine-gripped islet where his wound was made.
Entering a door-huge dictionary, he finds that clause
that stopped the war yesterday; his pulse starts the gavel
of hexametrical time, the V's of each lifted blade
pull from Connecticut, like the hammers of a piano
without the sound, as the wake, reaching gravel,
recites in American: *"Arma virumque cano . . ."*

Thalassa! Thalassa! The thud of that echoing blue
on the heart! Going to the Eastern shuttle at LaGuardia,
I mistook a swash of green-painted roof for the sea.
And my ears, that second, were shells that held the roar
of a burnished army scrambling down troughs of sand
in an avalanche of crabs, to the conch's horn in Xenophon.
My eyes flashed a watery green, I felt through each hand,
channel and vein, the startling change in hue
made by the current between Pigeon Point and Store
Bay, my blood royalled by that blue.
I know midsummer is the same thing everywhere—
Aix, Santa Fe, dust powdering the poplars of Arles,
that it swivels like a dog at its shadow by the Charles
when the footpaths swirl with dust, not snow, in eddies—
but my nib, like the beak of the sea-swift heads nowhere else;
to where the legions sprawl like starfish sunning themselves
till the conch's moan calls the slanted spears
of the rain to march on in Anabasis.
The sun has whitened the legions to brittle shells.
Homer, who tired of wars and gods and kings,
had the sea's silence for prologue and epilogue.
That old wave-wanderer with his drowsing gaze is
a pelican rocked on the stern of an empty pirogue,
a salt-grizzled gaffer, shaking rain from his wings.

Mud. Clods. The sucking heel of the rain-flinger.
Sometimes the gusts of rain veered like the sails
of dragon-beaked vessels dipping to Avalon
and mist. For hours, driving along
the skittering ridges of Wales, we carried the figure
of Langland's Plowman on the rain-seeded glass,
matching the tires with his striding heels,
while splintered puddles dripped from the roadside grass.
Once, in the drizzle, a crouched, clay-covered ghost
rose in his pivot, and the turning disk of the fields
with their ploughed stanzas sang of a freshness lost.
Villages began. We had crossed into England—
the fields, not their names, were the same. We found a caff,
parked in a thin drizzle, then crammed into a pew
of red leatherette. Outside, with thumb and finger,
a careful sun was picking the lint from things.
The sun brightened like a sign, the world was new
while the cairns, the castled hillocks, the stony kings
were scabbarded in sleep, yet what made me think
that the crash of chivalry in a kitchen sink
was my own dispossession? I could sense, from calf
to flinging wrist, my veins ache in a knot.
There was mist on the window. I rubbed it and looked out
at the helmets of wet cars in the parking lot.

The oak inns creak in their joints as light declines
from the ale-colored skies of Warwickshire.
Autumn has blown the froth from the foaming orchards,
so white-haired regulars draw chairs nearer the grate
to spit on logs that crackle into leaves of fire.
But they grow deafer, not sure if what they hear
is the drone of the abbeys from matins to compline,
or the hornet's nest of a chain saw working late
on the knoll up there back of the Norman chapel.
Evening loosens the moth, the owl shifts its weight,
a fish-mouthed moon swims up from wavering elms,
but four old men are out on the garden benches,
talking of the bows they have drawn, their strings of wenches,
their coined eyes shrewdly glittering like the Thames'
estuaries. I heard their old talk carried
through cables laid across the Atlantic bed,
their gossip rustles like an apple orchard's
in my own head, and I can drop their names
like familiars—those bastard grandsires
whose maker granted them a primal pardon—
because the worm that cores the rotting apple
of the world and the hornet's chain saw cannot touch the words
of Shallow or Silence in their fading garden.

A trembling thought, no bigger than a hurt
wren, swells to the pulsebeat of my rounded palm,
pecks at its scratch marks like a mound of dirt,
oval wings thrumming like a panelled heart.
Mercy on thee, wren; more than you give to the worm.
I've seen that pitiless beak dabbing the worm
like a knitting needle into wool, the shudder you give
gulping that limp noodle, its wriggle of completion
like a seed swallowed by the slit of a grave,
then your wink of rightness at a wren's religion;
but if you died in my hand, that beak would be the needle
on which the black world kept spinning on in silence,
your music as measured in grooves as was my pen's.
Keep pecking on in this vein and see what happens:
the red skeins will come apart as knitting does.
It flutters in my palm like the heartbeat thudding to be gone,
as if it shared the knowledge of a wren's elsewhere,
beyond the world ringed in its eye, season and zone,
in the radial iris, the targeted, targeting stare.

XXXVIII

Autumn's music grates. From tuning forks of branches,
small beaks scrape the cold. With trembling feather,
with the squeaking nails of their notes, they pierce me, plus
all the hauntings and evasions of gray weather,
and the river veining with marble despite their pleas.
Lunging to St. Martin's marshes, toward the salt breaks
corrugated by windy sunlight, to reed-whistling islets
the geese chevron, too high for a shadow. Over brown bricks
the soundless white scream of contrails made by jets
remains. Earlier and earlier the brownstones darken.
Now the islands feel farther than something out of the *Georgics*.
Maple and elm close in. But palms require translation,
and their long lines stiffen with dead characters.
Vergilian Brookline! By five, then four, the sun sets;
the lines of passengers at each trolley station,
waiting to go underground, have the faces of actors
when a play must close. Or yours, looking up from a desk,
from a play you hadn't reread for several years.
The look on the face of the sea when the day is finished,
or the seats in an empty theater, each one with its reasons
for what went wrong. They didn't know your language,
the characters were simple, there was no change of seasons
or sets. There was too much poetry. It was the wrong age.

The gray English road hissed emptily under the tires
since the woods still drizzled. The sound was like foam
mixed with island rain, but the rain was Berkshire's.
He said a white hare would startle itself like a tuft
on the road's bare scalp. But, wherever it came from,
the old word "hare" shivered like "weald" or "croft"
or the peeled white trunk with a wound in "atheling."
I hated fables. The wheezing beeches were fables,
and the wild, wet mustard. As for the mist, gathering
from the mulch of black leaves in which the hare hid
in clenched concentration—muttering prayers, bead-eyed,
haunch-deep in nettles—the sooner it disappeared
the better. Something branched in that countryside
losing ground to the mist, its old roads brown as blood.
The white hare had all of England on which to brood
with its curled paws—from the age of skins and woad,
from Saxon settlements fenced with stakes, and thick
fires of peat smoke, down to thin country traffic.
He turned on the fog lights. It was on this road,
on this ridge of earth long since swept bare
of his mud prints, that my bastard ancestor swayed
transfixed by the trembling, trembling thing that stood
its ground, ears pronged, nibbling him into a hare.

Mist soaps the motel room's window vigorously
every half hour. On tour, in this small town,
I feel like a drummer selling colored poetry
in samples bright as autumn, wondering if I sound
as if my voice were flattering the flag
with differences worse than a different R.
Through the cleaned glass I watch a sparrow perch
on a black branch with a tattered crimson fringe
on some tree I can't name, though I am sure
Sparrow could sing it like a citizen;
that sassy tilt knows where the answers are.
Like palms outlined against the hill's oasis,
the furniture yields to the evening.
Between the V made by your parted socks,
stare at the charred cave of the television.
Before its firelit image flickers on
your forehead like the first Neanderthal
to spend a whole life lifting nouns like rocks,
turn to the window. On a light-angled wall,
through the clear, soundless pane, one sees a speech
that calls to us, but is beyond our powers,
composed of O's from a reflected bridge,
the language of white, ponderous clouds convening
over aerials, spires, rooftops, water towers.

XLI

The camps hold their distance—brown chestnuts and gray smoke
that coils like barbed wire. The profit in guilt continues.
Brown pigeons goose-step, squirrels pile up acorns like little
    shoes,
and moss, voiceless as smoke, hushes the peeled bodies
like abandoned kindling. In the clear pools, fat
trout rising to lures bubble in umlauts.
Forty years gone, in my island childhood, I felt that
the gift of poetry had made me one of the chosen,
that all experience was kindling to the fire of the Muse.
Now I see her in autumn on that pine bench where she sits,
their nut-brown ideal, in gold plaits and *lederhosen,*
the blood drops of poppies embroidered on her white bodice,
the spirit of autumn to every Hans and Fritz
whose gaze raked the stubble fields when the smoky cries
of rooks were nearly human. They placed their cause in
her cornsilk crown, her cornflower iris,
winnower of chaff for whom the swastikas flash
in skeletal harvests. But had I known then
that the fronds of my island were harrows, its sand the ash
of the distant camps, would I have broken my pen
because this century's pastorals were being written
by the chimneys of Dachau, of Auschwitz, of Sachsenhausen?

Chicago's avenues, as white as Poland.
A blizzard of heavenly coke hushes the ghettos.
The scratched sky flickers like a TV set.
Down Michigan Avenue, slow as the glacial prose
of historians, my taxi crawls. The stalled cars are as frozen
as the faces of cloaked queues on a Warsaw street,
or the hands of black derelicts flexing over a fire-
barrel under the El; above, the punctured sky
is needled by rockets that keep both Empires high.
It will be both ice and fire. In the sibyl's crystal
the globe is shaken with ash, with a child's *frisson*.
It'll be like this. A bird cry will sound like a pistol
down the avenues. Cars like dead horses, their muzzles
foaming with ice. From the cab's dashboard, a tinny
dispatcher's voice warns of more snow. A picture
lights up the set—first, indecipherable puzzles;
then, in plain black and white, a snow slope with pines
as shaggy as the manes of barbarian ponies;
then, a Mongol in yak's skin, teeth broken as dice,
grinning at the needles of the silent cities
of the plains below him up in the Himalayas,
who slaps the snow from his sides and turns away as,
in lance-like birches, the horde's ponies whinny.

Tropic Zone / i

A white dory, face down, its rusted keel staining
the hull, bleeds under the dawn leaves of an almond.
Vines grip the seawall and drop like olive-green infantry
over from Cuba. This is my ocean, but it is speaking
another language, since its accent changes around
different islands. The wind is up early, campaigning
with the leaflets of seagulls, but from the balcony
of the guesthouse, I resist the return
of this brightening noun whose lines must be translated
into *"el mar"* or *"la mar,"* and death itself to *"la muerte."*
A rusty sparrow alights on a rustier rain gauge
in the front garden, but every squeak addresses
me in testy Spanish. "Change to a light shirt. A
walk on our beach should teach you our S's
as the surf says them. You'll recognize hovels,
rotting fishnets. Also why a white dory was shot
for being a gringo." I go back upstairs,
for so much here is the Empire envied and hated
that whether one chooses to say *"ven-thes"* or *"ven-ces"*
involves the class struggle as well. So, be discreet.
Changed to a light shirt, I walk out to Cervantes Street.
Shadow-barred. A water sprinkler or a tank approaches.
The corners are empty. The boulevards open like novels
waiting to be written. Clouds like the beginnings of stories.

ii

The sun is wholly up now; things are white or green:
clouds, hills, walls, leaves on the walls, and their shadows;
dew turns into dust on the quiet municipal cedars.
The sprinkler rolls past as "the wrong done to our fathers"
weeps along empty streets, down serene *avenidas*
named after stone poets, but the sprinkling only grows
traffic. When noon strikes the present-arms pose
of sentries in boxes before the Palace of Governors,
history will pierce your memory like a migraine;
but however their flame trees catch, the green winds smell
    lime-scented,
the indigo hills lie anchored in seas of cane
as deep as my island's, I know I would feel disoriented
in Oriente, my tongue dried to a coral stone.
Along white-walled, palm-splashed Condado, the breeze smells
of a dialect so strong it is not disinfected
by the exhausts of limousines idling outside the hotels,
while, far out, unheard, the grinding reef of the Morro
spits out like corals the indigestible sorrow
of the Indian, bits for the National Museum.
Blue skies convert all genocide into fiction,
but a man, drawn to the seawall, crouches like a question
or a prayer, and my own prayer is to write
lines as mindless as the ocean's of linear time,
since time is the first province of Caesar's jurisdiction.

iii

Above hot tin billboards, above Hostería del Mar,
wherever the Empire has raised the standard of living
by blinding high rises, gestures are made to the culture
of a remorseful past, whose artists must stay unforgiving
even when commissioned. If the white architectural mode is
International Modern, the décor must be the Creole's,
so, in a terra-cotta lobby with palms, a local jingle
gurgles of a new *cerveza,* frost-crusted and golden,
right next to a mural that has nationalized Eden
in vehement acrylics, and this universal theme
sees the golden beer, the gold mines, "the gold of their bodies"
as one, and our two tropics as erogenous zones.
A necklace of emerald islands is fringed with lace
starched as the ruffles of Isabella's bodice,
now the white-breasted Niña and Pinta and Santa María
bring the phalli of lances penetrating a jungle
whose vines spread apart to a parrot's primal scream.
Then, shy as the ferns their hands are bending, stare
fig-nippled maidens with faces calm as stones,
and, as is the case with so many revolutions,
the visitor doubts the murals and trusts the beer.

Noon empties balconies, but the arched eyebrows
of the plaza are not amazed at the continuum—
a fly drilling holes in a snoring peon's face,
the arched shade of patios humming with audible heat,
and long-fingered shadows retracting to a fist.
The statue's sword arm is tired, he'd like to dismount
from his leaf-green stallion and curl up in the shade
with the rest of his country. And that's how it was
in the old scenarios, a backdrop for the hectic
conscience of the gringo with his Wasp's rage at tedium,
but now in the banana republics, whose bunches of recruits
look green in fatigues, techniques of camouflage
have taught the skill of slitting stomachs like fruits,
and a red star without a sickle is stitched to a flag.
Now the women who were folded over wrought-iron
balconies like bedsteads, their black manes hanging down,
are not whores with roses but dolls broken in half.
On a wall a bleeding VIVA! hieroglyphs speeches
that lasted four hours in marathon dialectic.
Sand-colored mongrels prowl round a young Antigone,
her face flat as an axe of pre-Columbian stone.
At the movies, I still love it when gap-toothed bandidos laugh
in growling pidgin, then grin at the sudden contradiction
of roses stitching their guts. In colonial fiction
evil remains comic and only achieves importance
when the gringo crosses the plaza, flayed by the shadows of fronds.

V

"Wherever a thought can go back seventy years
there is hope for tradition in these tropical zones."
The old men mutter in white suits, elbows twitching like pigeons
on their canes, under the dusty leaves of the almonds
that grant them asylum from paths ruined by bicycles,
from machines with umbrellas dispensing franks and cones.
Their revolution is that things come in circles.
The socialists do not appreciate that.
But old almonds do, and there is appreciation
in the tilt of a cannon's chin to the horizon,
and applause from the seawall when a crash of lace
is like that moment of flamenco, *Ah, mi corazón,*
that moment of flamenco when the dancer's
heels rattled like gunfire and, above her tilted comb, her
clapping hands were like midnight on a clock!
For each old man, in his white panama hat,
there is no ideology in the light: this one
shakes his cane like a question without answers,
that one riddles the militia with his smiles,
another one leans backward in a coma
of silence—when lilies opened like Victrola horns,
when dusk spread feathers like a fighting cock,
and down the Sunday promenade for miles
the Civil Guard kept playing "La Paloma"
and gulls, like doves, waltzed to the gusting lace
and everyone wore white and there was grace.

vi

You've forgotten the heat. It could burn from a zinc fence.
Not even the palms on the seafront quietly stir.
The Empire sneers at all thoughts in the future tense.
Only the shallows of this inland ocean mutter
lines from another sea, which this one resembles—
myths of analogous islands of olive and myrtle,
the dream of the drowsing Gulf. Although her temples,
white blocks against green, are hotels, and her stoas
shopping malls, in time they will make good ruins;
so what if the hand of the Empire is as slow as
a turtle signing the surf when it comes to treaties?
Genius will come to contradict history,
and that's there in their brown bodies, in the olives of eyes,
as when the pimps of demotic Athens threaded the chaos
of Asia, and girls from the stick villages, henna-whores,
were the hetaerae. The afternoon tide ebbs, and the stench
of further empires—rising from berries that fringe
the hems of tyrants and beaches—reaches a bench
where clouds descend their steps like senates passing,
no different from when, under leaves of rattling myrtle,
they shared one shade, the poet and the assassin.

vii

Imagine, where sand is now, the crawling lava
of military concrete. Sprinkle every avenue with the gray
tears of the people's will. Tyranny brings over
its colonies this disorientation of weather. A new ogre
erects his bronzes over the parks, though the senate
of swallows still arranges itself on benches
for the usual agenda, and three men can still argue
under a changed street sign, but the streets are emptier
and the mouth dry. Imagine the fading hysteria
of peeling advertisements, and note how all the graffiti agree
with the government. You might say, Yes, but here are
    mountains,
park benches, working fountains, a brass band on Sundays,
here the baker still gives a special twist to the end
of his father's craft, until one morning you notice
that the three men talk softly, that mothers call
from identical windows for their children to come home,
that the smallest pamphlet is stamped with a single star.
The days feel longer, people resemble their cars
that are gray as their uniforms. In the millennium,
most men, at night, sleep with their eyes to the wall.

viii

If you were here, in this white room, in this hotel
whose hinges stay hot, even in the wind off the sea,
you would sprawl, knocked out by *la hora de siesta;*
you couldn't rise for the resurrection bell,
or the sea's gong ringing with silver, you'd stay down.
If you were touched, you'd only change that gesture
to a runner's in that somnambulist's marathon.
And I'd let you sleep. Things topple gradually
when the alarm clock, with its conductor's baton,
begins at one: the cattle fold their knees;
in the quiet pastures, only a mare's tail switches,
feather-dusting flies, drunk melons roll into ditches,
and gnats keep spiralling to their paradise.
Now the first gardener, under the tree of knowledge,
forgets that he's Adam. In the ribbed air
each patch of shade dilates like an oasis
to the tired butterfly, a green lagoon for anchor.
Down the white beach, calm as a forehead
that has felt the wind, a sacramental stasis
would bring you sleep, which is midsummer's crown,
sleep that divides its lovers without rancor,
sweat without sin, the furnace without fire,
calm without self, the dying with no fear,
as afternoon removes those window bars
that striped your sleep like a kitten's, or a prisoner's.

XLIV

I drag, as on a chain behind me, laterite landscapes—
streams where the sunset has fallen, the fences of villages,
and buffalo brooding like clouds of indigo. I pull the voices
of children behind me that die with the first star, the shapes
entering shops to buy kerosene, and the palms that darken
with the lines in my mother's hand. I cross the ditches
carefully like smoke, and the darkness steps into my head
like a mongrel under a house. The sunset has limits, the aching
fence posts rush past without waving, some are dead,
some faceless, black on the sky like erect kindling.
Green-black dusk, red earth, long horizons of cane fields
that shiver in the first breeze of night. Down a wet road
where the sun fell behind Chaguanas, my heart
is rattling. It is creaking like a rusty bullock cart
breaking the panes of sky in the road. It is in the red
glare of stiff cattle, in the boy who haies them with a switch
and the rattle of a bucket. Over these fields that the hoe scrapes
with its grating anguish, the furrows deepen. They are covered
with grass. They are mud. They spring up again in the rains
of November. I drag them behind me in chains.

What's missing from the Charles is the smell of salt,
though the thawed river, muscling toward its estuary,
swims seaward with the spring, then with strong shoulders
heaves up the ice. The floes crack like rifle fire.
Then gulls glitter like flakes, as keyed in pitch
as children's summer voices at the sea's edge
chasing the surf, pygmies with little spades who harry
a stumbling mastodon. But, like time, the sea
can't turn over on its side to die like a gray empire
brought down by its own weight. On satellite maps, a patch
of warring white says winter is fighting hard
to be remembered, but that it will melt from the memory
of even the Dakotas. The tines of willow branches
along the walks stand pronged for the spring planting.
When the light hits, they ring with the true pitch
of the Appalachian idyll. Then this empire's breath was
closer to the earth's. Through the iron net of a bridge,
the sunrise climbs with the leisure of a nuclear blast.
The Charles runs softly, carrying the shadow cast
by a black fisherman, his muscles smooth as boulders,
hurling his net at shoals of mackerel cirrus.

XLVI

Pale khaki fields of dehydrated grass
peer behind pointless fences—all the corn farms, straw.
A sky so huge, its haze is violet.
Over gelid canals, the wands of the pollard willows
fade when the highway branches into some small town;
spring, this Sunday, has come in a single stride
to Ohio, skipping the thaw. It's still February,
but the dazed hills couldn't tell you where winter went;
the light is rollering the white, facing side
of houses in Athens, Lancaster, and Wheeling,
polishing the stubble till it shines like brass.
The heat increases. Over Columbus, a second ceiling
coat of blue makes the day tropical. The law
that the light has broken winks from windows.
The spring was always free to violate
its vernal equinox, its shadow line,
but tirelessly a striped electric gate
patrolled by dogma and black-gloved police
decides where our devotions end and start,
and men in helmets block the arteries
of what was once the individual heart.
At a hot railroad crossing where we wait
till the light changes, a crossed black-and-white sign
says MARTIN'S FERRY. The wind-bright
stubble reaches Ohio's skyline, till the whole state
shines with the width of mercy in Jim Wright.

Gulls bicker with the spray, while the frigate birds circle
for hours, on one wingbeat, the reef where a pontoon rusts.
One year has finished its storms, and frightened men
have shielded their lives like lanterns from its gusts,
or fallen together in bonfires. But now blue spaces open
like gaps in the smoke, birds fold themselves in clefts
of rocks whose sand is raked clean of footprints. Ocean,
whose pride is that no man makes his mark on her,
still offers such places for the selfish pen,
and the brain's coral island has places where the polyp's
republic was built for us only—mesmerized grottoes
that wriggle with wave light, rockroses that whiten
with growing indifference driftwood or foundered ships.
After one year, you might call the commotion
of surf-cannoned sandbars war, and the stabbing thefts
the gulls beak each other for as all done in honor
of the gull-god. But there are islets where our shadow
is nameless, with minnows whose simile escapes
us as the anchor chain rattles from the bow.

Raw ocher sea cliffs in the slanting afternoon,
at the bursting end of Balandra, the dry beach's end,
that a shadow's dial wipes out of sight and mind.
White sanderlings race the withdrawing surf to pick,
with wink-quick stabs, shellfish between the pebbles,
ignoring the horizon where a sail goes out
like the love of Prospero for his island kingdom.
A grape leaf shields the sun with veined, orange hand,
but its wick blows out, and the sanderlings are gone.
Go, light, make weightless the burden of our thought,
let our misfortune have no need for magic,
be untranslatable in verse or prose.
Let us darken like stones that have never frowned or known
the need for art or medicine, for Prospero's
snake-knotted staff, or sea-bewildering stick;
erase these ciphers of birds' prints on sand.
Proportion benedict us, as in fables,
that in life's last third, its movements, we accept the
measurement of our acts from one to three,
and boarding this craft, pull till a dark wind
rolls this pen on a desktop, a broken oar, a scepter
swayed by the surf, the scansion of the sea.

XLIX

A wind-scraped headland, a sludgy, dishwater sea,
another storm-darkened village with fences of crucified tin.
Give it up to a goat in the rain, whose iron muzzle
can take anything, or to those hopping buzzards
trailing their torn umbrellas in a silvery drizzle
that slimes everything; on the horizon,
the sea's silver language shines like another era,
and, seasick of poverty, my mind is out there.
A storm has wrecked the island, the beach is a mess,
a bent man, crouching, crosses it, cuffed by the wind;
from that gap of blue, with seraphic highmindedness,
the frigate birds are crying that foul weather lifts the soul,
that the sodden red rag of the heart, when it has dried,
will flutter like a lifeguard's flag from its rusty pole.
Though I curse the recurrence of each shining omen,
the sun will come out, and warm up my right hand
like that old crab flexing its fingers outside its hole.
Frail from damp holes, the courageous, pale bestiary
of the sand seethes, the goat nuzzles, head bent
among flashing tins, and the light's flood tide
stutters up to a sandbar in the estuary,
where, making the most of its Egyptian moment,
the heron halts its abrupt, exalted stride—
then a slow frieze of sunlit pelicans.

I once gave my daughters, separately, two conch shells
that were dived from the reef, or sold on the beach, I forget.
They use them as doorstops or bookends, but their wet
pink palates are the soundless singing of angels.
I once wrote a poem called "The Yellow Cemetery,"
when I was nineteen. Lizzie's age. I'm fifty-three.
These poems I heaved aren't linked to any tradition
like a mossed cairn; each goes down like a stone
to the seabed, settling, but let them, with luck, lie
where stones are deep, in the sea's memory.
Let them be, in water, as my father, who did watercolors,
entered his work. He became one of his shadows,
wavering and faint in the midsummer sunlight.
His name was Warwick Walcott. I sometimes believe
that his father, in love or bitter benediction,
named him for Warwickshire. Ironies
are moving. Now, when I rewrite a line,
or sketch on the fast-drying paper the coconut fronds
that he did so faintly, my daughters' hands move in mine.
Conches move over the sea floor. I used to move
my father's grave from the blackened Anglican headstones
in Castries to where I could love both at once—
the sea and his absence. Youth is stronger than fiction.

Since all of your work was really an effort to appease
the past, a need to be admitted among your peers,
let the inheritors question the sibyl and the Sphinx,
and learn that a raceless critic is a primate's dream.
You were distressed by your habitat, you shall not find peace
till you and your origins reconcile; your jaw must droop
and your knuckles scrape the ground of your native place.
Squat on a damp rock round which white lilies stiffen,
pricking their ears; count as the syllables drop
like dew from primeval ferns; note how the earth drinks
language as precious, depending upon the race.
Then, on dank ground, using a twig for a pen,
write Genesis and watch the Word begin.
Elephants will mill at their water hole to trumpet a
new style. Mongoose, arrested in rut,
and saucer-eyed mandrills, drinking from the leaves,
will nod as a dew-lapped lizard discourses on "Lives
of the Black Poets," gripping a branch like a lectern for better
delivery. Already, up in that simian Academe,
a chimp in bifocals, his lower lip a jut,
tears misting the lenses, is turning your *Oeuvres Complètes*.

I heard them marching the leaf-wet roads of my head,
the sucked vowels of a syntax trampled to mud,
a division of dictions, one troop black, barefooted,
the other in redcoats bright as their sovereign's blood;
their feet scuffled like rain, the bare soles with the shod.
One fought for a queen, the other was chained in her service,
but both, in bitterness, travelled the same road.
Our occupation and the Army of Occupation
are born enemies, but what mortar can size
the broken stones of the barracks of Brimstone Hill
to the gaping brick of Belfast? Have we changed sides
to the mustached sergeants and the horsy gentry
because we serve English, like a two-headed sentry
guarding its borders? No language is neutral;
the green oak of English is a murmurous cathedral
where some took umbrage, some peace, but every shade, all,
helped widen its shadow. I used to haunt the arches
of the British barracks of Vigie. There were leaves there,
bright, rotting like revers or epaulettes, and the stenches
of history and piss. Leaves piled like the dropped aitches
of soldiers from rival shires, from the brimstone trenches
of Agincourt to the gas of the Somme. On Poppy Day
our schools bought red paper flowers. They were for Flanders.
I saw Hotspur cursing the smoke through which a popinjay
minced from the battle. Those raging commanders
from Thersites to Percy, their rant is our model.
I pinned the poppy to my blazer. It bled like a vowel.

There was one Syrian, with his bicycle, in our town.
I didn't know if he was a Syrian or an Assyrian.
When I asked him his race, about which Saroyan had written
that all that was left were seventy thousand Assyrians,
where were sixty-nine thousand nine hundred and ninety-nine?
he didn't answer, but smiled at the length of our street.
His pupils flashed like the hot spokes of a chariot,
or the silver wires of his secondhand machine.
I should have asked him about the patterns of birds
migrating in Aramaic, or the correct
pronunciation of wrinkled rivers like "Tagus."
Assyria was far as the ancient world that was taught us,
but then, so was he, from his hot-skinned camels and tents.
I was young and direct and my tense
was the present; if I, in my ignorance,
had distorted time, it was less than some tyrant's
indifference that altered his future.
He wore a white shirt. A black hat. His bicycle
had an iron basket in front. It moved through the mirage
of sugar-cane fields, crediting suits to the cutters.
Next, two more Syrians appeared. All three shared a store
behind which they slept. After that, there was
a sign with that name, so comical to us, of mythical
spade-bearded, anointed, and ringleted kings: ABDUL.
But to me there were still only seventy thousand
Assyrians, and all of them lived next door
in a hot dark room, muttering a language whose sound
had winged lions in it, and birds cut into a wall.

The midsummer sea, the hot pitch road, this grass, these shacks
   that made me,
jungle and razor grass shimmering by the roadside, the edge
   of art;
wood lice are humming in the sacred wood,
nothing can burn them out, they are in the blood;
their rose mouths, like cherubs, sing of the slow science
of dying—all heads, with, at each ear, a gauzy wing.
Up at Forest Reserve, before branches break into sea,
I looked through the moving, grassed window and thought
   "pines,"
or conifers of some sort. I thought, they must suffer
in this tropical heat with their child's idea of Russia.
Then suddenly, from their rotting logs, distracting signs
of the faith I betrayed, or the faith that betrayed me—
yellow butterflies rising on the road to Valencia
stuttering "yes" to the resurrection; "yes, yes is our answer,"
the gold-robed Nunc Dimittis of their certain choir.
Where's my child's hymnbook, the poems edged in gold leaf,
the heaven I worship with no faith in heaven,
as the Word turned toward poetry in its grief?
Ah, bread of life, that only love can leaven!
Ah, Joseph, though no man ever dies in his own country,
the grateful grass will grow thick from his heart.

Index of First Lines

Imagine, where sand is now, the crawling lava XLIII, *vii*
In the other 'eighties, a hundred midsummers gone XVIII
It touches earth, that branched diviner's rod IX

Midsummer stretches beside me with its cat's yawn VI
Mist soaps the motel room's window vigorously XL
Mud. Clods. The sucking heel of the rain-flinger XXXV
My double, tired of morning, closes the door XI

No subtle fugues between black day, black night X
Noon empties balconies, but the arched eyebrows XLIII, *iv*

On the quays of Papeete, the dawdling white-ducked colonists XIX, *i*
Our houses are one step from the gutter. Plastic curtains VII

Pale khaki fields of dehydrated grass XLVI
Perhaps if I'd nurtured some divine disease XXIX

Raw ocher sea cliffs in the slanting afternoon XLVIII
Rest, Christ! from tireless war. See, it's midsummer XXII

Since all of your work was really an effort to appease LI
So what shall we do for the dead, to whose conch-bordered XVI
Something primal in our spine makes the child swing XXVIII

Thalassa! Thalassa! The thud of that echoing blue XXXIV